MYSTERIES
OF
MOONS
AND
MOON PHASES

by Ellen Labrecque

Capstone Captivate is published by Capstone Press, an imprint of Capstone.
1710 Roe Crest Drive
North Mankato, Minnesota 56003
www.capstonepub.com

Library of Congress Cataloging-in-Publication Data is available on the Library of Congress website.
ISBN: 978-1-4966-8078-5 (library binding)
ISBN: 978-1-4966-8717-3 (paperback)
ISBN: 978-1-4966-8171-3 (eBook)

Summary: Text describes moons and moon phases, and mysteries about them.

Image Credits
Alamy: Science History Images, 22; NASA, 10, 26; NASA's Scientific Visualization Studio, 19 (Bottom); NASA: Goddard Space Flight Center Scientific Visualization Studio, 9, JPL/University of Arizona/University of Idaho, 24; Science Source: Science Photo Library/Mark Garlick, 28; Shutterstock: Alhovik, 18, 19 (Top), BlueRingMedia, 17, Jaime Enrique, 13, Josef Hanus, 21 (Top), Juergen Faelchle, Cover, Kateryna Omelianchenko, 21 (Bottom), Keith Publicover, 6, Klagyivik Viktor, 12, Mathias_R, 5, Paolo G, 16, Pikul Noorod, 27, Siberian Art, 11, Tom Reichner, 15, Vadim Sadovski, 25

Design Credits
Shutterstock: Anna Kutukova, Aygun Ali

Editorial Credits
Editor: Hank Musolf; Designer: Sara Radka; Media Researcher: Jo Miller; Production Specialist: Laura Manthe

All internet sites appearing in back matter were available and accurate when this book was sent to press.

Direct Quotations
Page 26, from July 20, 1969. NASA article "One Small Step," www.hq.nasa.gov/alsj/a11/a11.step.html

Printed and bound in China. PO5070

TABLE OF CONTENTS

Words in **bold** appear in the glossary.

CHAPTER 1

THE POWER OF THE MOON

Does a full moon make us do strange things? This is what people believed a long time ago. The word *lunacy* means "crazy." This comes from the word *lunar*. *Lunar* means "moon" in Latin. Full moons are awesome to see! But you don't have to worry: they don't cause people to act strangely. Moons do a lot of other things, though. Scientists know a lot about Earth's moon. But some things remain a mystery. Scientists are always learning about our moon as well as other moons in space.

A full moon lights up the night sky.

Earth's gravity keeps our moon in orbit.

Moons are **satellites**. They **orbit** a planet instead of the sun. Earth has one moon orbiting it. Some other planets have many moons. There are at least 193 moons in our **solar system**. Scientists believe Earth's moon came into being about 4.5 billion years ago. A giant **asteroid** crashed into Earth. A large chunk of the asteroid flew into space. The Earth's **gravity** locked the chunk in Earth's orbit. This became our moon. Earth is 8,000 miles (12,874 kilometers) all the way around. The moon is 2,200 miles (3,540 km). It is our nearest space neighbor, just 240,000 miles (386,242 km) away. We are more than 92 million miles (148,059,648 km) away from the sun!

MYSTERY FACT

The planet Jupiter has the most moons in our solar system. It has 63 moons.

Our moon looks like a giant ball of Swiss cheese. This is because the moon is covered in **craters**, or deep holes. **Meteors** caused the craters. These pieces of rocks flew through space and crashed into our moon. Unlike Earth, the moon has no **atmosphere** to protect itself. Without an atmosphere, it can't deflect these rocks away. The biggest crater on the moon is named the South Pole-Aitken Basin. It is half the width of the United States and almost 5 miles (8 km) deep.

In 2019, scientists discovered something else. A giant and mysterious blob sits 180 miles (290 km) beneath the basin. Scientists think the blob could be made of metal left over from an asteroid. Researchers are studying the blob to find more about it.

the far side of the moon

Tsiokovskly crater

Mare Moscoviense crater

Jules Verne crater

Aitken Basin

Does this moon photo show craters?
If so, can you point them out?

CHAPTER 2

THE MOON'S ORBIT

The moon takes 27.3 days to orbit Earth. This is the same amount of time it takes the moon to rotate on its **axis**. This is called a **synchronous orbit**. As a result, we only ever see one side of the moon from Earth. The side of the moon we always see is called the near side. The side we never see is called the dark side. That side isn't any darker than the side we see, though. It gets the same amount of sunlight. Some scientists have seen the dark side of the moon from a spacecraft. They even took a photograph of it in 1959. It is more rugged and has more craters than the near side.

dark side of the moon, as photographed from the *Apollo 16*

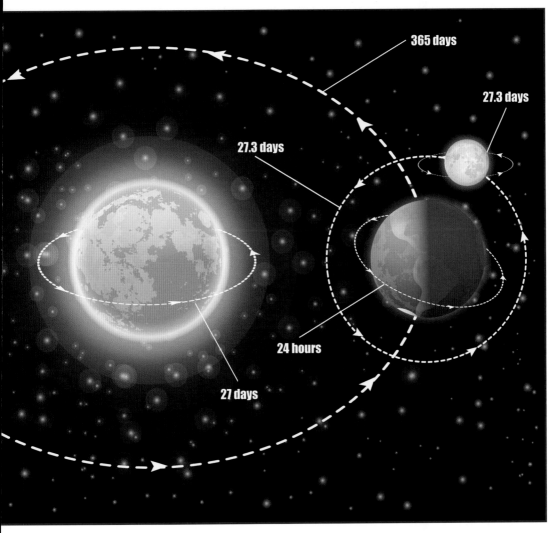

365 days

27.3 days

27.3 days

24 hours

27 days

interplay of sun,
Earth, and moon

When it is near the horizon, the moon appears larger.

Sometimes the moon appears bigger in the sky than at other times. The moon looks especially big when it is low in the sky. This means it is near the **horizon**. This is called the moon's illusion. It just looks bigger because you can compare it to things like mountains. But when it is up high in the sky, you can't compare it to anything. It doesn't look as big when it seems to be alone in the sky.

The moon is not always the same distance from Earth when it orbits. At its nearest point, it is 238,855 miles (384,399 km) away. At its farthest point, it is 269,906 miles (434,371 km) away.

When it is high in the sky, the moon appears smaller.

CHAPTER 3

SHAPE-SHIFTER

On some nights, you look up into the sky and the moon is full. On other nights, you look up and the moon is just a sliver. Does the moon change shape? No. But the moon's appearance is based on the sun. The moon doesn't have any of its own light. As Earth rotates around the sun, the sun's light reflects against the moon in different ways. This is known as the **lunar cycle**. The different ways we see the moon from Earth are called phases. There are eight phases of the lunar cycle.

MYSTERY FACT

The moon orbits the Earth at a speed of 2,300 miles (3,701 km) per hour.

phases of the moon

The first phase of the lunar cycle is called the new moon. During the new moon phase, the Earth side of the moon is completely dark. This is because the moon is between Earth and the sun. As the moon rotates around Earth, the sun lights it more and more. This is called a waxing moon. When Earth is between the sun and the moon, we see a full moon. The entire Earth side of the moon is lit. As the moon continues to move, it becomes less lit. This is called a waning moon. When the moon is less than half lit, it is called a crescent moon. When the moon is more than half lit, it is called a gibbous moon.

crescent moon

Phases of Earth's Moon

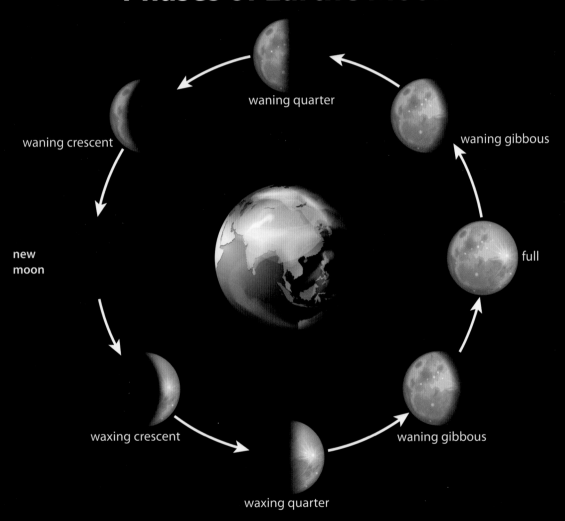

waning quarter

waning gibbous

waning crescent

full

new
moon

waxing crescent

waning gibbous

waxing quarter

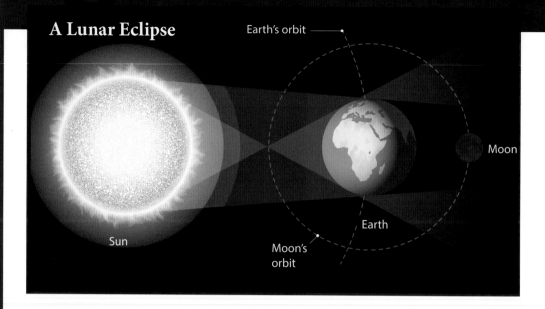

A Lunar Eclipse

Earth's orbit

Sun

Moon's orbit

Earth

Moon

An **eclipse** is when an object in space is partially or fully hidden. This is because of the placement of another object. There are two common types of eclipses. They are a lunar eclipse and a solar eclipse.

A lunar eclipse is when Earth's shadow covers up the moon. This happens when Earth is directly between the sun and the moon. A solar eclipse is when the moon is directly between Earth and the sun. It is blocking sunlight from reaching us. This might seem impossible. The moon is a lot smaller than the sun. It happens because the moon is so much closer to Earth than it is to the sun. It is like if you hold your thumb up to the sky. You can block out entire mountains or stars, even though they are much bigger than your thumb.

A Solar Eclipse

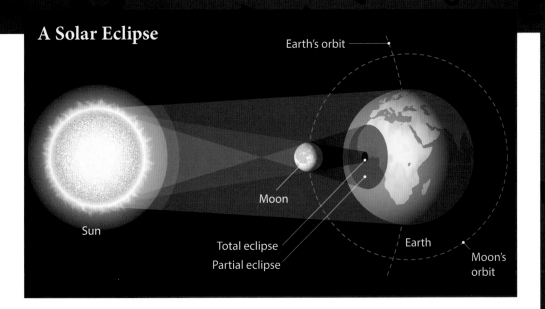

- Earth's orbit
- Moon
- Sun
- Total eclipse
- Partial eclipse
- Earth
- Moon's orbit

THE PATH OF TOTALITY ON AUGUST 21, 2017

THE PATH OF TOTALITY

In the summer of 2017, the United States experienced a total solar eclipse. This is when the sky in parts of Earth goes dark. The moon appears to completely cover the sun. The total eclipse went across the United States. It covered a path 70 miles (113 km) wide from Oregon to South Carolina. It was called the Path of Totality. A total eclipse occurs somewhere on Earth about once every 18 months. But it can only be witnessed by people in a small part of Earth.

CHAPTER 4

THE WAY OF THE TIDE

Did you know the moon controls the ocean's tides? When the ocean is high, we call it high tide. When it is low, it is called low tide. Because of gravity, the moon and Earth pull toward each other. When the moon pulls on Earth, our water moves. The side of Earth nearest the moon builds up the water in a wave. A wave is also being formed on the other side of Earth. The moon is pulling Earth from the water on that side too.

Bay of Fundy, high tide

Bay of Fundy, low tide

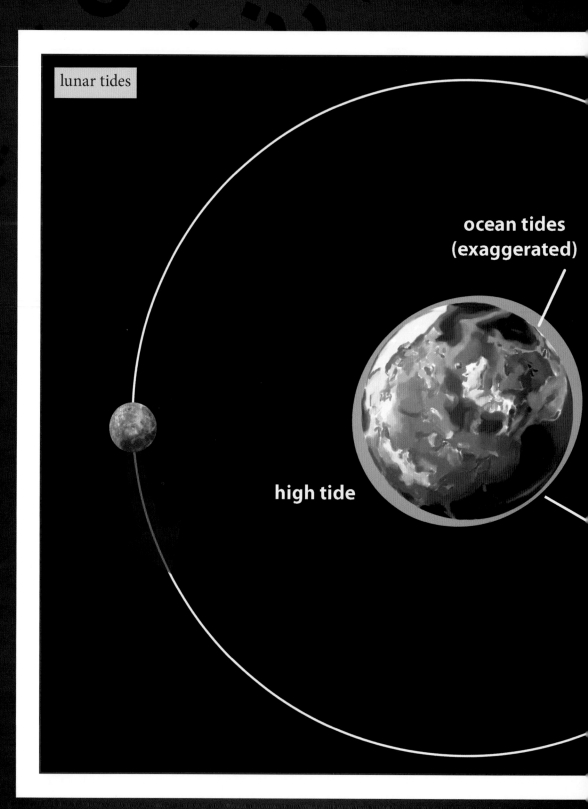

lunar tides

ocean tides
(exaggerated)

high tide

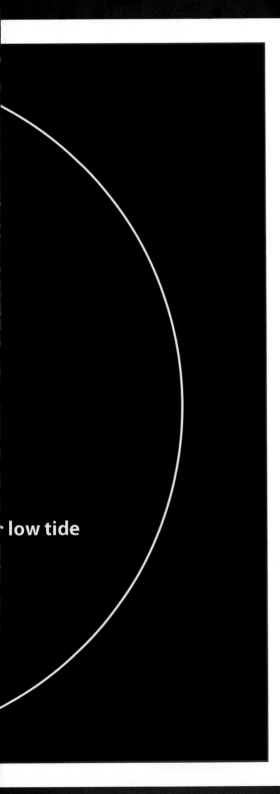

low tide

Where the pull from the moon is the strongest, it causes high tides. Where the pull from the moon is weaker, it causes low tides. The moon is spinning and rotating around Earth. Earth is spinning and rotating around the sun. This causes Earth to have several tides a day. Some coastal areas have two high tides and two low tides each day. Other places have one of each. The highest tides in the world can be found in the Bay of Fundy in Canada.

OTHER MOONS

Besides Earth's moon, there are 192 other moons in our solar system. Most of the other moons go around the planets Jupiter, Saturn, Uranus, and Neptune. They have more than 100 moons between the four of them.

Saturn has 53 moons. One, named Titan, is special. Titan is the only known moon in the universe with an atmosphere. This means Titan has different kinds of weather. It also can protect itself from asteroids, so it doesn't have a lot of craters.

Titan

Jupiter and its moons

CHAPTER 6

THE FUTURE OF THE MOON

Our moon continues to fascinate us. It controls our tides. It can block our sun even though it is so much smaller than it. We don't know everything about the future of the moon. We do know the moon is moving 1.4 inches (3.8 centimeters) away from Earth every year. When the moon was first formed, it was six times closer than it is today. Does this mean the moon will disappear from Earth one day? Because of gravity, the moon will never move away entirely from us. This is good. We would miss our moon!

MAN ON THE MOON

The moon is the only other place in space besides Earth where a man has walked. The first person to walk on the moon was Neil Armstrong. Armstrong walked on the moon on July 16, 1969. When he took his first steps, he said, "That's one small step for a man, one giant leap for mankind."

People will continue to admire the moon for years to come.

Someday, scientists think bases could be built on the moon, where people would live.

Astronomers work every day to learn more about space and all its moons. The United States is planning to send astronauts back to the moon again in 2024. Scientists want to continue to study it. Maybe someday people will even live on the moon! In the meantime, there is one thing we know for sure. We are just beginning to understand the mysteries of the moon, space, and the stars.

GLOSSARY

asteroid (AS-tuh-roid)—rocky object in space

atmosphere (AT-muhs-feer)—gases that surround planets or other objects in space

axis (AK-siss)—a real or imaginary line through the center of an object, around which the object turns

crater (KRAY-ter)—cup-shaped holes on the moon

eclipse (ih-KLIPS)—when an object in space is partially or fully hidden because of the placement of another object

gravity (GRAV-i-tee)—the force that pulls objects together

horizon (huh-RYE-zuhn)—the boundary between Earth and the sky

lunar cycle (LOO-ner SYE-kuhl)—the phases of the moon

meteor (MEE-tee-ur)—a meteoroid that has entered Earth's atmosphere

orbit (OR-bit)—a curved path around another object in space, usually the sun

satellite (SAT-uh-lite)—a natural body that circles around a planet

solar system (SAT-uh-lite)—the Sun and the objects that move around it

synchronous orbit (SING-kruh-nuhs OR-bit)—when the orbit of the moon takes the same amount of time as its spin

READ MORE

Bizony, Piers. *Moonshots: 50 Years of NASA Space Exploration Seen Through Hasselblad Cameras.* Minneapolis: Voyageur, 2017.

Koestler-Grack, Rachel. *Space Travel from Then to Now.* North Mankato, MN: Amicus Ink, 2020.

Jenkins, Steve. *Solar System: By the Numbers.* Boston: HMH For Young Readers, 2020.

INTERNET SITES

NASA: The Moon
https://www.nasa.gov/moon

National Geographic Kids: Facts About the Moon!
nationalgeographic.com/science/2004/07/moon-facts/

Space.com: Moon Facts: Fun Information About the Earth's Moon
space.com/55-earths-moon-formation-composition-and-orbit.html

INDEX